THE COUNTRYSIDE IN THE PAST

Laurie Bolwell & Clifford Lines

The Countryside

The Countryside in the Past
Farming the Land
Country Crafts and Industries
Villages Today
Recreation and Tourism
The Countryside under Threat

Cover *This medieval scene shows sheep being sheared.
At this time wool was Britain's chief source of wealth.*

Frontispiece *An English country lane in the nineteenth century.
'The Green Lane' by Myles Birket Foster.*

Editor: Philippa Smith

First published in 1987 by
Wayland (Publishers) Limited
61 Western Road, Hove
East Sussex BN3 1JD, England

© Copyright 1987 Wayland (Publishers) Limited

British Library Cataloguing in Publication Data
Bolwell, L.H.
The countryside in the past. — (The countryside)
1. Great Britain—Rural conditions
Britain—Social life and customs—Juvenile literature
I. Title   II Lines, C.T. III series
941'009'734   DA110

ISBN 0 85078 933 8

Phototypeset by D.P. Press, Sevenoaks, Kent
Printed in Italy by G. Canale & C. S.p.A., Turin
Bound in the U.K. by the Bath Press, Avon

Contents

6

History in the Landscape

The scenery that we see from a car or railway carriage has undergone many changes in its long history, altered by generations of people who have lived and worked in the countryside. These people have left us clues as to what life was like in the past. Sometimes changes have been slow, like the gradual cutting down of the woodland; sometimes they have been rapid, like the building of a new housing estate. Often one single country scene can tell us about many different events in its history.

The small Essex village of Pleshey provides us with a direct link to the Norman conquerors who lived there nine hundred years ago. It also contains evidence of other periods in its history. The unusual shape of the village shows up clearly in the aerial photograph, opposite. The hill in the middle is 18 metres high and man-made. It is a mound, or motte, on which a castle was built by a Norman lord called Geoffrey de Mandeville. He may have used an existing mound dating from prehistoric times. The wooden castle has gone but the defences are still to be seen. There is a bailey, or inner defence platform, with a raised edge and a moat. The outer defence was a circular ditch, which still surrounds the village. It once had a thick hedge for extra protection. The bridge between the motte and the bailey was built in the fifteenth century.

Not far from the mound (below right) there is a Norman church, and close by there are marks on the ground which show where a religious college once stood. It was built by Richard II's uncle, the Duke of Gloucester.

The village houses are fairly recent, but the road which curves around the mound may go back to Saxon or earlier times. The land outside the medieval perimeter was once divided into open fields and cultivated in strips. Later it was enclosed to make rectangular fields with hedges forming the field boundaries. Today many of these hedges have been pulled up to give large open fields suitable for modern farm machinery.

In this book you will read about how the British countryside has changed and about the clues to these changes which can still be found today.

Left *The small village of Pleshey, near Chelmsford in Essex, has many features which can tell us about its history.*

Chapter 1

Early Settlements

THE EARLIEST SETTLERS

If we could go back in time some 8,000 years we would find quite a different countryside from the one we see today. At that time most of Britain was covered by a blanket of forests, with marshland around the coast and near the rivers. The small groups of people who lived in these forests survived by hunting, fishing and food gathering.

The first settlers to farm in Britain came from Europe over 5,000 years ago. They used tools made of wood, with flint or stone heads, to cut down trees and clear

Left   *A typical Celtic farming settlement, around 500 BC.*

Below   *The remains of Maiden Castle, Dorset, originally a Stone Age camp.*

some of the land for farming. Because they used stone heads on their tools this period is called the Stone Age. They kept sheep, cattle and pigs, and grew a form of wheat in small rectangular fields. These fields can still be seen in some places. Only a few traces of their homes remain, but the countryside contains many of their stone tombs.

In time many other groups of people from Europe settled in Britain. About 700 BC the first of the Celts arrived from Western Europe. These people knew how to make iron tools, so this period is called the Iron Age. During the Iron Age the British countryside contained many small villages, hamlets and farmsteads, with farmland covering much of the lower ground. The houses were circular with a framework of wooden poles. Walls were made of wattle and the roofs were thatched.

In some parts of Britain we can still see the circular banks and ditches of hill forts which Iron Age people built. Many of these hill forts contained large settlements protected by wooden ramparts. In Scotland circular stone towers, called brochs, inside walled court-yards, served a similar purpose.

Above *The remains of a broch at Carloway in the Hebrides.*

Right *During the Iron Age, a Scottish broch would have looked something like this.*

THE ROMANS

When the Romans invaded Britain in 54 BC, they found a countryside with many small farms and settlements and patches of woodland. A haphazard network of tracks linked the settlements.

During the Roman occupation of the next four hundred years, farming flourished because food was needed by the Roman army and by the increasing number of people living in towns. The main crops grown were wheat and barley, to

Above *The remains of Hadrian's Wall.*

Below *The Romans built Hadrian's Wall from the Solway Firth in the west, to the mouth of the River Tyne in the east, as a defence against the northern British tribes.*

A Roman country villa. Many of these were run as large farms.

feed the soldiers and their horses. Sheep and cattle were reared for their meat, wool and leather. We know from the examination of ancient rubbish pits that beans, peas, cabbages, carrots, parsnips and various types of fruit were also grown. Because the Romans used a heavy type of plough which was difficult to turn at the end of a furrow, land was cultivated in long, narrow strips which resulted in long fields.

The Romans planned a road network with London as its centre. The main Roman towns and ports were linked by straight roads, except where a hill or other obstruction formed an obstacle. As well as transporting goods, these straight roads were intended for rapid movement of soldiers to check outbreaks of unrest. The roads were built on a bank to help drainage, and surfaced with local stone.

The way of life of country people changed little during the Roman occupation. Some farmers did well from the increased demand for their produce, and with their extra wealth they built extensions to their homes, using Roman ideas and decorations. Some wealthy Romans built houses in the country-side, which were similar to the villas they had left behind in Italy.

The remains of one of the largest and most lavish villas can be seen in Gloucestershire at Chedworth. It had over thirty rooms, central heating by means of hot air in channels under the floor, and richly decorated walls. Floors in the more important rooms were made of thousands of small pieces of stone or tile, called mosaic.

Widecombe-in-the-Moor grew up in a sheltered Dartmoor valley.

WHERE VILLAGES GREW UP

Why did villages grow up in some places and not in others? To answer this question we must think about the things the early settlers needed and try to imagine what the countryside was like at that time. Today, underground drains lead water from the fields and roads into ditches and streams. In earlier times these drains did not exist and much low-lying land was wet and marshy. Villages grew up on well-drained sites such as valley slopes, ridges of sand or gravel, or low hills where there was enough level land to build homes.

Shelter was also important, particularly in uplands such as the Pennines, Dartmoor, Wales and Scotland. Sites exposed to high winds, heavy rain and winter snow were avoided.

Villages developed where the people could grow crops and keep animals. Good farmland was essential, and the lighter soils which could be ploughed fairly easily were preferred to the heavy and sticky clays. Pastureland was also needed as grazing for livestock.

Settlements developed where there was suitable land for villagers to grow crops.

Both the villagers and their animals needed fresh water, so many settlements were built close to a spring or where water could be obtained easily by digging a well. Timber was needed as a fuel and as a building material. Carrying firewood long distances was exhausting and wasted energy.

In parts of the country where all these needs were close at hand villages flourished.

Some villages, such as Wilmington shown below, grew up on well-drained land near a spring, and stretch across a variety of soils.

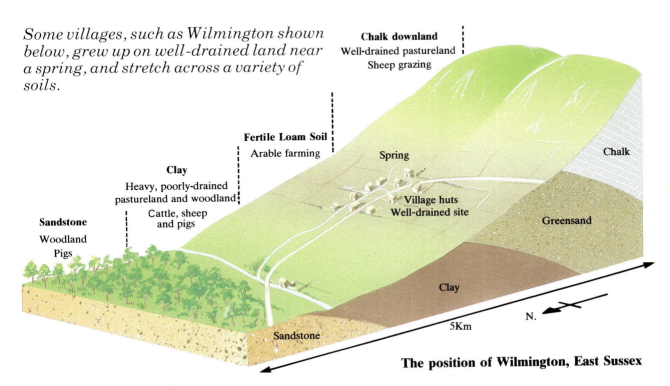

The position of Wilmington, East Sussex

A SAXON VILLAGE

Ploughing the land in spring.

After the Romans left Britain in the fifth century AD, groups of people from North Germany, known today as the Saxons, came to Britain. They were farmers and chose to settle on the farmlands of the English lowlands. The Celts retreated to Wales, Cornwall and the Highlands of Scotland.

The Saxons cultivated large fields which were bordered by paths or low banks. The fields were ploughed in strips, with half the land left fallow each year so that it had time to regain its fertility. Wheat and other grain crops were sown as well as peas and beans. The villagers rented their strips of land from the local lord and much of the work on the land was done in teams. There were also larger farms owned by lords who employed managers, called 'reeves', to look after them.

We have accounts, written at the time, of what farm workers on these farms were expected to do in each of the four seasons.

The Saxons were skilled carpenters and their houses were built of wood, turf and straw. A home consisted of a large room with partitions at one end.

Many Saxon settlements were the foundations of today's villages and towns.

Winter	Plough, make cattle stalls and pig pens, cut wood, thresh grain.
Spring	Plough, sow seed for crops, dig ditches, sow madder (plant producing a red dye), woad (plant producing a blue dye) and linseed.
Summer	Break up fallow land, shear sheep, weed, general repairs.
Autumn	Reap and mow, dig up woad, gather in crops, plough.

Many English villages still have Saxon names, for example places with names ending in 'ton', 'ing' and 'ham'. 'Ton' means an enclosure, 'ing' means 'descendants of' or 'followers of', and 'ham' means the home of a chief or tribe. Some examples are Kingston-upon-Thames (the king's farmstead), Hastings (the followers of Haesta), Buckingham (the home of the followers of Bucc). Although Saxons built new villages, they also renamed some which had already existed for hundreds of years.

Do you know how the town or village where you live got its name?

Chapter 2

The Middle Ages

DOMESDAY ENGLAND

The Norman invasion in 1066 brought considerable changes both to the countryside and to the ways of life of the people. As a reward for their help in defeating the Anglo-Saxons, the Norman barons were given land by the new King, and gradually took control of the countryside. We know a great deal about this land and its people because in 1086 King William ordered a survey to be made. He wanted to know the value of the land owned by his subjects because his wealth and power came from a land tax. This survey still exists and is called the *Domesday Book*.

Officials were sent to different parts of the country to record the name and owner of each manor; the number of people and the size of their holdings; the amount of woodland, pasture, meadow and arable land; the number of plough teams (eight oxen to one plough), and the value of the estate. These facts were not recorded as accurately as they would be today because there was no standard system of measuring and different groups of officials made the survey. The areas which are now Wales, Scotland and the far north of England were not included in the survey because they were not under William's control.

The *Domesday Book* gives us a very detailed picture of what the English countryside was like in 1086. It was a land of villages and

The Bayeux Tapestry, made in the 11th or 12th century, depicted the Norman conquest of England. This section shows the building of Hastings Castle.

Haymaking — the grass was cut with long scythes and raked into large heaps. It was later carted away to the lord of the manor's barn, to be stored for the winter.

large estates. The south and east had the highest populations and the largest amount of arable land. Poor sandy areas, the Fens, moorlands and heavy clay regions had few, if any, settlements. Some regions, such as Cannock Chase in Staffordshire, central Sussex and Kent, and the New Forest were wooded, but most of the countryside was dotted with farms, hamlets and villages, giving England a population of between 1,500,000 and 2,000,000.

Lower Brockhampton, Herefordshire, a medieval manor house surrounded by a moat.

MEDIEVAL VILLAGES

In a medieval village there were two important buildings, the church and the manor house. These two buildings can still be seen in some villages, whereas the wooden huts of the villagers have long since disappeared.

The Normans added sections to many Saxon churches and also built new churches. Local stone was used when possible. The church was the finest building that local craftsmen could create and that the people could afford. Each year one-tenth of the villagers' crops and animals had to be given to the church as a tithe (tenth). This tax made the clergy wealthy and powerful.

Manor houses were timber framed and usually consisted of a large hall with a high roof which led to other smaller rooms. The hall was the dining and living area of the manor and the centre of its

Villagers' huts were usually made of wattle and daub, with a thatched roof. The more prosperous tenants had separate sheds for their animals, but poorer people lived in single-roomed huts, with one end partitioned off for their livestock.

social and business activities. Some manor houses were surrounded by a moat, probably to make them look more important, although they were also useful for drainage and as a source of fish.

We know the villagers' huts were very poor buildings compared with the manor house. They were built of wattle, with low, thatched roofs and earth floors. The life of a villager was hard and often cut short by disease. When he or she died, burial was in an unmarked grave, whereas the lord of the manor had a tomb inside the church.

The two places in the village where the villagers could meet were the church, which was used for local festivities as well as for religious services, and an open space called the green. The village green had many uses. It provided grazing for animals, made a suitable marketplace and was a recreation area for archery and other games.

ABBEYS AND MONASTERIES

The abbeys and monasteries of medieval times were important centres for religion, learning, farming, health care and industries such as milling and brewing. They also provided travellers with food and a place to sleep. The Normans built cathedrals in large towns but most abbeys and monasteries were built in the heart of the countryside.

The earliest abbeys in Britain were founded by St Benedict in the seventh century. The monks grew fruit, vegetables and herbs to support themselves. Later, abbeys owned large areas of land and monks worked alongside their tenants, the village people.

One group of monks, the Cistercians, settled in remote regions, such as the uplands of Yorkshire and the Welsh borders. They cleared waste land and raised sheep. In North Yorkshire the village of Old Byland was knocked down by the monks to give them a site for their abbey (Rievaulx Abbey), and another village built on the moor. At the end of the twelfth century there were about 140 monks and over 500 lay brothers at Rievaulx. The large-scale rearing of sheep made Cistercian monasteries extremely rich.

In medieval times, monks made a living from the land.

Melrose Abbey in Scotland. The surrounding land was ideal for sheep farming.

Some of the Cistercian monks from Rievaulx founded another abbey at Melrose in Scotland in 1136. It was built of local red sandstone and became one of the richest abbeys in Scotland. Wool from the abbey's sheep was sold in the market at Berwick.

All the religious houses were closed down during the reign of King Henry VIII, when England changed from being a Roman Catholic country and became Protestant. Rievaulx Abbey was closed in 1539 and Melrose Abbey was destroyed by an English army in 1547.

The ruins of some of these great abbeys can still be found today. From their peaceful country surroundings it is hard to imagine how busy they once were. Some had a population the size of a large town.

The remains of Grey Abbey in Northern Ireland, a Cistercian monastery founded in 1193.

THE OPEN-FIELD SYSTEM

Villagers ploughing their strips of land.

In Medieval times, fields in the Midlands and southern and eastern England were not surrounded by hedges as they are now. The land was divided into long strips. Hedges were only to be seen around fields in the west of England, where the land was left as pasture.

Many village families only owned or rented about 12 hectares of land. Each family could not afford to keep a team of oxen, so ploughing, like many other jobs, was carried out by groups of villagers. A special court, called the Court Leet, decided what work was to be done.

The system of ploughing turned over the ground into a series of ridges and furrows. A number of these side by side made up a strip. Each strip was about 200 metres long, making the old English measure of a furlong (furrow long). This length was supposed to be the distance an ox team could pull a plough without resting. The strips were part of a large field and there were at least two of these fields in each village. This allowed one field to be cultivated while another was manured and left fallow. Medieval farmers did not have the variety of crops and artificial fertilizers we use today to allow for crop rotation.

Ridge and furrow patterns can still be seen in many parts of

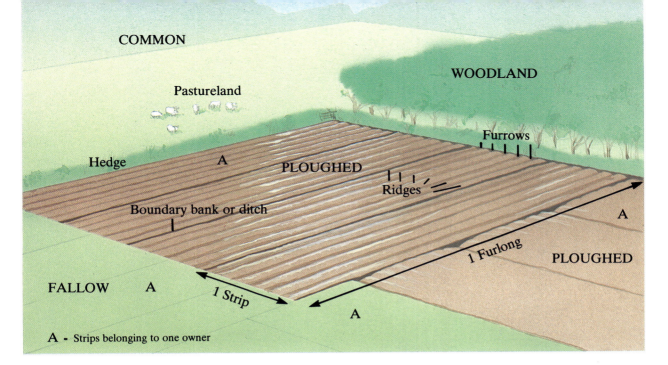

COMMON

WOODLAND

Pastureland

Hedge   A   PLOUGHED

Furrows

Ridges

Boundary bank or ditch

1 Furlong   PLOUGHED

A

FALLOW   A   1 Strip

A

A - Strips belonging to one owner

Above *Each villager's strips were scattered across the fields so that some were on cultivated land and some on fallow. Scattered strips also shared out the good and bad soils more fairly.*

England but the open-field system has almost disappeared.

Much of Scotland, Wales and the north of England had another pattern of farming. One field near the village was continuously cultivated with the heavy use of manure. This was called the infield. Further away an area of rough pasture, known as the outfield, was used for grazing, with portions being cropped for short periods and then left to recover. Some crofts in Scotland use a similar system of farming today.

Right *At Laxton, in Nottinghamshire, an aerial photograph reveals how the land is still farmed in strips.*

ROADS

The Saxon invaders inherited the earlier road networks and added short sections of their own called 'ways', but they were not great road builders like the Romans. However, the road system was good enough for King Harold at York to travel with his army about 300 kilometres in a week, to fight the Norman invaders near Hastings in 1066.

The increase in the number of towns and market centres after the Norman invasion put an added strain on the roads. Road repairs were the responsibility of the parishes and estates through which they passed, and travellers constantly complained about the mud and pot-holes. Some roads were made dangerous by outlaws and highwaymen, who threatened

Above *The straight road on the right is Ermine Street, in Lincolnshire. Originally built by the Romans, it has been used for centuries and is still used today.*

Poor road conditions often made travelling difficult.

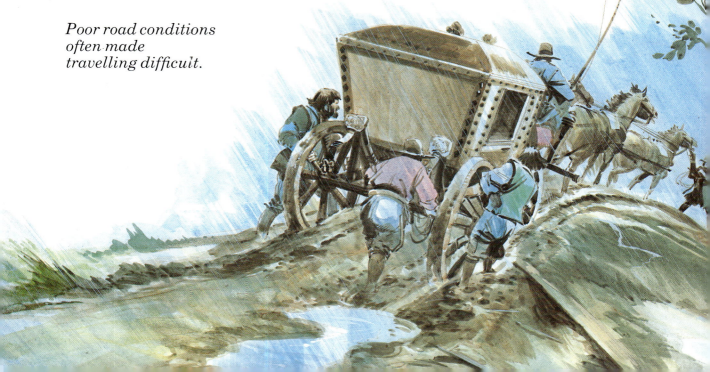

Pilgrims in the 14th century, travelling to Canterbury.

the travellers. A law in 1285 ordered a section on either side of the highway to be cleared of bushes and places where villains could hide. Local lords and town officials often asked travellers to pay a toll to help pay for the upkeep of roads. They were also asked for money when crossing certain bridges.

A common sight on some roads were herds of cattle or sheep being driven long distances to be sold at fairs. Other travellers to be seen were the King and his court, judges going to local trials, and pilgrims making a trip to a saint's tomb or holy place.

Heavy goods were often carried by river because the roads were so bad, and some towns, such as Gainsborough on the River Trent, were important inland ports.

MARKET CENTRES

During the thirteenth century there was an increase in the number of people living in towns. Some villages grew large enough to become towns, and more than sixty-five new towns were built. Villagers sold their grain and other farm produce to merchants from the towns and in return bought pots and pans, cloth and other town-made goods. Most buying and selling at this time was done at markets. There were few shops but each large village and town had a market place.

Local lords had to obtain a charter from the King to hold a market, and over 2,500 charters were granted during the thirteenth century.

Markets were held in neighbouring villages on different days of the week, so that merchants could move from one to another. For

Traders at a medieval market place.

An old market cross in the centre of Castle Combe, in Wiltshire.

country people market day was the highlight of the week. Because most people walked to market these centres grew up close to one another. On average, people living in a village without a market would have to walk about 10 kilometres to reach one, a journey which would take about two hours on the poor roads of those days. In some places a covered market hall was built, or a market cross set up as a symbol of fair trading to the people who bought and sold there. More often, stalls were set up in the main street. A number of villages and towns owe their wide high streets to the fact that sheep or other farm animals were sold there in the Middle Ages.

The travelling traders were usually based in towns, and spent their time moving around the countryside from one market to another by pack horse or covered cart. Some merchants bought produce such as wool to sell abroad. Towns such as Market Harborough in Leicestershire, and Wickham Market in Suffolk, have names which remind us of their past importance.

Chapter 3
The Changing Landscape

ENCLOSURE AND CLEARANCE

When foreign visitors arrive in Britain by air, one of their first impressions is of the neat patchwork of different coloured fields below. Many of these fields have existed for less than 300 years.

By the year 1700, only about half the land then used for growing crops was 'enclosed' by ditches, hedges and walls to form small fields. The rest was made up of huge open fields which had existed since the time of the Normans. As well as arable land there were about 4,000,000 hectares of moor, heathland and barren land. The open fields were worked by villagers who also had the right to graze their animals on the common land — the heathland and moors.

The North Yorkshire Moors. Walls divide up areas which were once common land.

However, in the eighteenth century, Parliament appointed special commissioners to visit villages and decide how the land should be enclosed. The landscape we see today was created by these commissioners. Each villager's land was relocated in one area. Squarish fields were made which were separated by hedges or walls, with more or less straight roads crossing the countryside. Enclosure made it possible for the wealthier landowners to use new farming methods, and so get higher yields from the land. However, many small farmers could not compete, and were forced to sell their land and become tenant farmers or labourers.

When the Scots noticed how prosperous English farmers had become, the lairds, who owned the land in Scotland, were keen to copy the new ideas. Land in Scotland was enclosed with dykes and hedges; woodlands were planted, marshes drained and new roads built. The new system destroyed the old farming pattern. In the Scottish Highlands the lairds tried to make the land more productive by turning the hillsides into sheep walks. To achieve this, the crofting families had to be evicted, and as a result many Scots emigrated to Canada and New Zealand in search of a better way of life.

Above *The Enclosure Acts caused many poor people to leave their villages to look for work in the towns.*

Below *A derelict croft in Caithness, Scotland.*

Trapping wildfowl was once common practice in the Fens.

DRAINING THE FENS

Today, the Fens are one of England's richest farming regions, yet once they were a region of swamps and pools and useless for farming. People lived on the islands of higher land, and made a living by fishing, fowling, cutting reeds for thatch, and keeping geese — the feathers were used for making pillows and pens. At one time many people used stilts to keep their feet dry as they walked through these wetlands. Floods were caused by the silting up of the Fenland rivers.

Other wetlands were equally useless — the Somerset Levels, the 'mosses' of Lancashire, parts of east Yorkshire, and the Isle of Axholme in north Lincolnshire. Today all these areas can be used for farming.

The wetlands were changed when landowners realised that many more hectares of land could be cultivated if the region was drained. In the Middle Ages some land had been reclaimed in a simple way. Low brushwood fences were built on marshes at river mouths. The mud and silt carried in by high tides was then trapped behind the fences. Plants soon found a foothold on the silt and within ten years the new land could be used as pasture for cattle and sheep.

Later, more scientific methods were used. The world experts were the Dutch, who had reclaimed much of their own country from the sea. They boasted, 'God made the world but the Dutch made Holland.' In 1630, the Earl of Bedford employed a Dutchman, named Cornelius Vermuyden, to start draining the Fens. Dykes and channels were dug. Later, windmills were built to pump water into the new drainage ditches. The Fens became a 'little Holland'.

Fenmen did not like the changes and sometimes opened up the new sluice gates to flood the land again. But the newly-drained areas soon became valuable farmland, which had to be protected from river floods and the sea at all costs.

Above *There are still many windmills to be seen. This one is at Cley-next-the-Sea in Norfolk.*

Below *In the mid-eighteenth century, a dyke was cut to drain Whittlesea Mere in the Fens.*

The Rolle aqueduct — part of the Torridge Canal in Devon.

CANALS AND RAILWAYS

The Industrial Revolution of the eighteenth century created many new industries in Britain. However, they could only thrive and grow if the large quantities of raw materials needed by the factories, and the goods produced, could be moved swiftly and cheaply. The roads of the time were very poor and the wagons very slow. Packhorses and small river boats were no longer adequate. Canals, and then railways, proved to be better means of transport.

The 'Canal Age' began in 1761 with a 4½-kilometre canal built from Worsley to Manchester. The builder, James Brindley, invented ways of taking canals through difficult country. He cut tunnels through hills and built aqueducts across rivers and valleys. When factory owners saw how successful this first canal was they planned and built more. Most of our canals were built between 1790 and 1834.

As industry continued to grow and expand, a faster and more efficient system than the canals was needed. The invention of the steam locomotive, followed by the success of George Stephenson's first railway line, joining Stockton to Darlington in 1825, marked the beginning of the 'Railway Age'. Dozens of different companies built railways across the countryside. Goods could be carried much more cheaply by rail than by road or canal, and by 1850 it was possible for the public to travel by train to most parts of Britain.

The canals and railways added new features to the countryside. Both canals and railways passed through rural areas, and lock-keepers' houses, warehouses, level crossings with keepers' houses, bridges, railway stations and halts were all built in what had once been areas of farmland. Most of these features can be found today, even though some canals have fallen into disuse, and some railway tracks have been dismantled.

Many of the small rural communities through which trains passed grew in importance. Trains

Blasting rocks on a section of the London-Birmingham railway, 1837.

were faster and cheaper than stage-coaches, so for the first time people could afford pleasure trips. In 1871, Clacton-on-Sea in Essex had a population of about 1,000. The railway came in 1882, and by 1900 Clacton had grown into a town of 7,500 people, many of them catering for London holidaymakers.

The Liverpool-Manchester railway, 1831.
Top: first class and mail.
Bottom: second and third class.

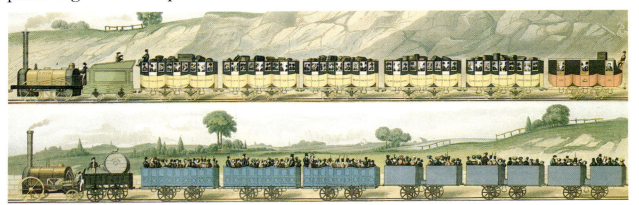

Chapter 4

Buildings in the Countryside

VILLAGE HOUSES

In the past, the homes of farmworkers and others who lived in the countryside were built from materials which could be obtained locally, although special building stone and other expensive materials might be brought in for important buildings such as the church or manor house.

This dependence upon local materials gave the villages in different parts of Britain, such as Cornwall, Kent and Scotland, their own distinctive character.

Just over 100 years ago village houses began to look more alike. This was the result of the building of railways, and then modern roads, which made it possible to send building materials from one part of the country to another. As a result many village houses were re-roofed with fashionable slates. New village houses were built with bricks from the chief brickwork regions, such as Bedfordshire.

A typical Cornish house, built from the local stone with a slate roof.

Crofters' cottages in the Hebrides. The roofs are thatched or covered in turf.

Today, village houses are being modernized with new building materials. For instance, timber weatherboarding is being replaced with plastic, which does not rot and does not need painting. If you visit a village, have a look around — it should be possible to see how the building techniques have changed over the years.

Weatherboarded houses in Tenterden, Kent.

STATELY HOMES

One of the attractions which brings millions of foreign tourists to Britain each year are the stately homes of old aristocratic families which are now open to the public.

Woburn Abbey, a stately home in Bedfordshire.

One famous stately home is Woburn Abbey in Bedfordshire. The Duke of Bedford's family, the Russells, have lived there for nearly 500 years. The first Russell to own it was a trusted courtier of King Henry VIII. When the King died, he was given the abbey as a present. At the time the abbey was in ruins — the last Abbot had been hanged for criticizing the King, and the monks had been evicted. In 1746, the then Duke of Bedford decided to have a large house built where the abbey had once stood.

Because families like the Russells of Woburn and the Salisburys of Hatfield House had links with royalty and the government, and played a big part in important historical events, their homes contain many valuable reminders of the past.

A detail from 'Woburn Sheepshearing', painted in 1804.

The famous landscaped grounds of Stourhead, in Wiltshire.

The wealthy owners of these grand country houses also owned the surrounding land. Visitors to stately homes will see beautiful parkland, but the grounds were not always like this. The owners hired designers, such as William Kent or Capability Brown, to 'landscape' the grounds. For instance, a bleak, marshy valley might be turned into a park with lakes and temples, and dotted with large ornamental trees and groups of flowering shrubs. One owner even went as far as diverting a river, while at Chatsworth, in Derbyshire, the sixth Duke of Devonshire had the village of Edensor destroyed and rebuilt elsewhere, so that it would not be visible from the house.

Fletching Church, in East Sussex.

CHURCHES

Just as stately homes, palaces and castles are living museums containing the history of the famous British families, village churches provide clues to the ordinary people who lived in the countryside.

Fletching Church is not famous, but like thousands of other village churches in Britain it contains a wealth of information about the history of the village. We can tell from the building style in the tower that the Saxons built a church here. We know too that local materials were used, because on the oldest parts of the roof there are Horsham tiles, stone tiles named after a Sussex town where they were once produced.

Inside the church there are the tombs of important families who once lived in the village and owned

A hatchment inside Fletching Church.

contains memorials to villagers who lost their lives in two world wars and in the service of the British Empire.

The church was once the centre of village life and there were other village buildings connected with it. As well as the vicarage there were almshouses, in which elderly people could live in comfort in the days before the National Health Service, old age pensions and council housing. In Fletching there was 'glebeland' owned by the church, and the rent from this land was used to keep the church in good repair. Opposite the church is the village school which also belonged to the church.

Village customs and lifestyles have now changed and fewer people look to the church as the centre of their lives. However, many people still go to church on special occasions, such as weddings, and at Easter and Christmas.

the surrounding land. Hanging inside the church are the armour and spurs of a medieval knight. There are also memorial tablets called 'hatchments'.

In the graveyard, the names on the gravestones show that some families have lived in the local area for centuries, and, like every other parish church, Fletching also

Tombstones in Fletching churchyard belonging to different generations of the same family.

Chapter 5
Village Life 100 Years Ago

An elderly countryman who lived in a village 100 years ago had probably seen more changes in his lifetime than anyone who had lived there before. He had seen transport by stage-coach and wagon give way to canals and railways. He had seen steam-powered machinery replace men and horses in jobs that had previously been unchanged for hundreds of years. As a farmworker he had been very poor all his life.

If he had lived in one of the southern counties of Britain, such as Dorset, his home as a young man might have looked like the cottage in the picture. The main food for the family was potatoes, and the sackful against the wall was their chief food supply. Although

The interior of a Dorset labourer's cottage in 1846.

The whole family helped at harvest time.

farmworkers were provided with cottages by the farmers, their condition was often very poor and it was difficult to persuade the owner to spend money on improvements.

When higher wages and better jobs could be found in the new factories and on the railways, country people began to move into towns. As farmworkers became scarce their wages slowly improved. The table on the right shows a typical farmworker's wages in 1893 and how the family spent its money each week. As you can see there was very little left over to buy extra food, clothes, shoes, or even treats for the children. At hay time and harvest time everybody in the village worked. The 4p a day earned by the women was saved and used to pay for boots and warmer clothes for the winter, or a few extras for Christmas.

Families were also expected to help the farmer with other jobs. This would include picking stones off the fields, scaring birds from the crops, weeding, and thinning out fields of turnips. Even school had to take second place to the needs of the farm. Children stayed away from school until their harvest work was over. If the harvest was late the summer holidays had to be lengthened.

Weekly bill for a family of five in 1893	
Income per week	
Father	55p
Elder son	25p
	80p
Expenditure per week	
Bread	31p
Bacon	7½p
Cheese	5p
Butter	6p
Tea and sugar	9p
Flour	2½p
Tobacco	1½p
Sundries	4p
Club subscription	4p
	70½p

Chapter 6
Things to do

THE LANDSCAPE IN THE PAST

There are many ways of finding out about history in the countryside. If you live in a town or city you can find information from books in the library. Find out more about the people in the early chapters of this book — the Romans and the villas they built, the Norman castles, the remains of ancient settlements, and life in Saxon times.

If you live in a town you can find out about the buildings which are common to both town and countryside; for example, old castles, ancient churches and other religious buildings. Some have undergone many changes over the years, and have a fascinating history. Use the information that you collect, such as postcards, photographs and so on, to make a booklet called *The Landscape in the Past*.

Manorbier Castle, in South Wales, was built by the Normans in the 12th century. The castle was never attacked, but because of its isolation it was often used by smugglers.

STATELY HOMES

Ask people you know, which of the stately homes they have visited is their favourite. Ask them why they like it best. From their answers work out what attracts visitors to country houses. Design a brochure which you think would attract even more visitors to Woburn Abbey, or to Chatsworth (above), or to a famous house you know well.

PICTURE QUIZ

The sixteenth-century woodcut on the right shows plants being cultivated.

Do you know the name of these plants?

Do you know what is made from these plants?

Buildings like this can still be seen in the countryside.

What are these buildings called?

What are they used for?

Where in Britain are you most likely to see them?

Have you guessed the link between these two pictures?

A HOUSE SURVEY

Choose a village near your home. If you live in a city you might pick a small area which was once a village but which has now been swallowed up by the city.

Choose an old house to study. You may be able to interview the people who live in the house to find out as much as you can.

Here are some questions to investigate:

What building materials were used and which were obtained locally?

Is the house typical of the building styles used in your part of the country?

Draw sketches or take photographs of the house to show its main features.

What evidence is there that the house has been altered or modernized since it was first built? Write a report on what you find.

Imagine you were a reporter visiting this cottage 150 years ago. What questions would you ask the family about themselves and their way of life?

DOMESDAY SURVEY

In 1985, thousands of schools took part in a modern Domesday survey. Find out if a school near you took part in this survey. What did they record about the local area?

Recently, the *Domesday Book* has been translated and published in forty volumes. Find out if your local library has the volume relating to your county, and see what it says about your town or village and the surrounding area.

COUNTRYSIDE MUSEUMS

An increasing number of open-air museums are now being set up in Britain. They have all kinds of exhibits relating to the countryside in the past, from steam trains and old farm machinery to reconstructions of iron-age settlements and rare breeds of farm animals.

Find out if there is a countryside museum in your area. Perhaps your school can arrange a visit.

Visitors at the North of England Open-Air Museum at Beamish, in County Durham.

Glossary

Abbot   The head of an abbey.

Aqueduct   An artificial channel which carries water, or a canal, in the same way as a bridge carries a road.

Arable land   Land which is suitable for ploughing and for growing crops.

Bailey   The outer defences of a Norman castle, usually in the form of a mound protected by a wall. The space inside the wall was used as living quarters for troops, and stables for horses and cattle.

Broch   A fortified circular tower built for defence in Scotland.

Croft   A small area of farmland worked by a tenant farmer in the Highlands and islands of Scotland.

Domesday Book   The record of a land survey made in 1086 by the King's officials. It contains information about each estate and farm in the country at that time, including such things as the sizes of fields and woods, and numbers and types of livestock.

Evict   To turn out a person or people, especially from a house or land.

Fallow   Ploughed land that is left unseeded and uncultivated for a time (usually a year) in order to restore its fertility.

Hatchment   A diamond-shaped tablet of stone displaying the coat of arms of a dead person.

Heathland   An open lowland area of uncultivated land which has infertile soils. Usually it is covered with heather, gorse, rough grass and scattered trees.

Industrial Revolution   The change in Britain which came about in the eighteenth and nineteenth centuries, when the country became a manufacturing nation instead of a farming nation.

Infield   A field close to a village or farm which is manured to keep it fertile and is cultivated year after year.

Laird   A Scottish landowner.

Lay brothers   Religious men who had taken vows to be obedient and not marry, but who did not have the duties of a monk.

Manor   An estate which consisted of part of a village or a number of villages. It was owned by the lord of the manor and contained land worked by villagers.

Market cross   A stone cross erected in a market place. It was used to seal bargains between sellers and buyers. It was also a reminder to the traders that they should be honest.

Mosaic   A design or picture made up of many small pieces of coloured marble, glass or other stones.

Motte   The mound or hill on which a Norman castle was built. The motte was usually surrounded by a water-filled moat with a bridge leading to the bailey.

Open-field system   The system of cultivation in which large fields were bordered by a path, ditch or bank and not a hedge. Villagers worked strips of land in the open fields. Each year one or two strips were ploughed to grow crops and one was left fallow.

Outfield   An area of wasteland, some distance from a village or farm, used as pasture or for short-term cultivation.

Raw materials   The materials which are used by an industry to make the finished product. For example, iron ore, coal and limestone are the main raw materials in the steel industry.

Silt   Sand and mud deposited by a river in its own channel, in a harbour or in the sea.

Thresh To separate grain from straw by beating it with a flail.

Toll A tax paid in order to cross a toll bridge or use a toll road.

Villa A large Roman house, often built around a courtyard. Villas in Britain were built in the same style as those in Italy.

Wattle Woven branches, or strips of wood, which formed the base on which mud was plastered to make the walls of houses in the Middle Ages.

Weatherboarding Horizontal boards on the wall of a house. Each board overlaps the next in order to throw off the rain and keep the house dry.

Books to Read

Boyden, Peter B., *The Children's Book of Domesday England* (Kingfisher, 1985)

Butcher, T.K., *Country Life* (Batsford, 1970)

May, Robin, *Alfred the Great and the Saxons* (Wayland, 1984)

May, Robin, *William the Conqueror and the Normans* (Wayland, 1984)

Pluckrose, Henry, *Seen in Britain* (Mills & Boon, 1977)

Ross, Stewart, *A Medieval Serf* (Wayland, 1985)

Ross, Stewart, *A Saxon Farmer* (Wayland, 1985)

Ross, Stewart, *Chaucer and the Middle Ages* (Wayland, 1985)

Watson, Lucilla, *A Celtic Family* (Wayland, 1987)

Whitlock, Ralph, *Landscape in History* (Wayland, 1984)

Picture Acknowledgements

Aerofilms Ltd 6, 23 (bottom), 24 (top); Mark Bergin 9 (right), 14/15 (bottom); The Bridgeman Art Library *frontispiece*, 37, 41; Britain on View (BTA/ETB) 10 (top), 43 (top); Bruce Coleman 29 (bottom) (Geoff Doré); Mary Evans Picture Library 25, 29 (top), 33 (both); Duncan Fraser 38, 39 (both); Highlands and Islands Development Board 9 (top); Michael Holford 16, 42; John James 26; Cliff Lines 27, 43 (bottom); The Mansell Collection 40; The National Trust Photographic Library (R. Surman) 18; Northern Ireland Tourist Board 21 (bottom); North of England Open Air Museum, Beamish 45 (bottom); Ann Ronan Picture Library 30, 32, 45 (top); Scottish Tourist Board 21 (top), 35 (top); By kind permission of the Marquess of Tavistock, and the Trustees of the Bedford Estates 36 (both); Malcolm S. Walker 13 (bottom), 23 (top); Wayland Picture Library *cover*, 8 (both), 14 (top), 17, 19, 20, 22, 31 (bottom) 43 (middle); Gerry Wood 10 (bottom), 11, 13 (top), 24 (bottom); Jennie Woodcock 28, 44; Tim Woodcock 31 (top), 35 (bottom); ZEFA 12, 34.

Index